EXPLORE BIOMES

GRASSLAND BIOMES

BY LAURA PERDEW

Kids Core
An Imprint of Abdo Publishing
abdobooks.com

abdobooks.com

Published by Abdo Publishing, a division of ABDO, PO Box 398166, Minneapolis, Minnesota 55439.

Printed in the United States of America, North Mankato, Minnesota.
052023
092023

THIS BOOK CONTAINS RECYCLED MATERIALS

Cover Photo: Shutterstock Images
Interior Photos: James Hager/Robert Harding Picture Library/SuperStock, 4–5; Shutterstock Images, 8, 13, 25 (grass), 25 (prairie dog, falcon, coyote, pronghorn), 26, 28 (bison, wildflower), 28 (rock), 28–29, 29 (prairie dog, pheasant, pronghorn); Zack Frank/Shutterstock Images, 10–11; Aizar Raldes/AFP/Getty Images, 15; Steve Pfost/Newsday LLC/Newsday/Getty Images, 16; Theron Stripling III/Shutterstock Images, 18–19; Greg Birkett/Shutterstock Images, 20; Wild Media/Shutterstock Images, 22; Rafal Szozda/Shutterstock Images, 23; Albert Beukhof/Shutterstock Images, 24; Chalintra B./Shutterstock Images, 25 (grasshopper)

Editor: Angela Lim
Series Designer: Ryan Gale

Library of Congress Control Number: 2022949086

Publisher's Cataloging-in-Publication Data

Names: Perdew, Laura, author.
Title: Grassland biomes / by Laura Perdew
Description: Minneapolis, Minnesota: Abdo Publishing Company, 2024 | Series: Explore biomes | Includes online resources and index.
Identifiers: ISBN 9781098291105 (lib. bdg.) | ISBN 9781098277284 (ebook)
Subjects: LCSH: Grasslands--Juvenile literature. | Biotic communities--Juvenile literature. | Habitats--Juvenile literature. | Life zones--Juvenile literature. | Grassland animals--Juvenile literature. | Grassland plants--Juvenile literature. | Grassland ecology--Juvenile literature.
Classification: DDC 577--dc23

CONTENTS

Dung beetles can be found in grasslands around the world.

CHAPTER 1

A HOME ON THE PLAINS

A bison feeds on the grasses of the Great Plains. This grassland stretches across the central part of North America from Texas into Canada. The bison gets **nutrients** from the grasses. It leaves behind dung once it is finished digesting its food.

A nearby dung beetle smells the fresh animal droppings. The beetle breaks off a chunk from the pile and forms it into a ball. Then the beetle uses its powerful back legs to roll the dung.

Dung beetles eat and live in dung. They also lay their eggs in it. The beetles reduce the waste on grasslands. They return leftover nutrients to the soil. They move seeds in the dung as they roll it. These beetles also loosen the soil as they make tunnels or bury balls of dung. This lets oxygen in. It allows water to flow through the soil more easily. These beetles improve soil health and boost **biodiversity**. Grassland plants and animals benefit from the work of dung beetles.

Grasslands

Grasslands are one of Earth's biomes. Biomes are communities of plants, animals, and nonliving things. Each biome has different plants and animals that live there. Biomes also have different soils and climates. The plants and animals in a biome are **adapted** to living there. Each has a role in the biome.

Keystone Species

Keystone species play important roles in their biomes. They may limit the populations of other plants and animals. They may help other species survive. Keystone species keep a biome healthy. Bison are a keystone species. Their dung improves soil health. They are food for other grassland animals.

Nutrient-rich soil in grasslands supports many types of grasses and wildflowers.

More than 20 percent of the land on Earth is grassland. Grasslands are on every continent except Antarctica. They are large, open areas. They are mostly flat.

Grasslands have different names depending on where they are. In North America, they are called prairies. Tropical grasslands in Africa and other places are called savannas. Grasslands are also called steppes, Pampas, velds, plains, and Cerrado.

Grasses and wildflowers are the main plants in this biome. **Precipitation** affects how tall plants grow. In some grasslands, the grass is short. In others, it can grow taller than a person! Some grasslands have shrubs and small trees. These biomes include many types of animals.

Explore Online

Visit the website below. Does it give any new information about grasslands that wasn't in Chapter One?

Grasping Grasslands

abdocorelibrary.com/grassland-biomes

High mountains can block rainfall. This creates dry conditions that allow grasslands to develop.

CHAPTER 2

TYPES OF GRASSLANDS

Grasslands form in the center of continents where there is not much rainfall. They get more precipitation than deserts. But they do not get enough for forests to grow.

There are two types of grasslands. They are temperate grasslands and tropical grasslands. Summers on temperate grasslands are warm. Winters can be very cold. These grasslands get 20 to 35 inches (51–89 cm) of rain per year. The Great Plains are temperate grasslands. There are few trees. Other temperate grasslands are found in South America, Europe, and Asia.

Tropical grasslands are called savannas. There are savannas in Africa, Australia, South America, and India. Savannas are warm year-round. They have a dry season and a wet season. The wet season lasts for six to eight months. Savannas get up to 50 inches (127 cm) of rain per year. This is enough rainfall for small trees and shrubs to grow.

Tropical grasslands cover much of northern Australia.

Wildfires

Both temperate and tropical grasslands experience wildfires. In temperate grasslands, fires are more likely during the summer. In tropical grasslands, the dry season has a greater risk of fire than the wet season. Usually, these fires are started by lightning. Others are caused by human activity.

Loss of Grasslands

Grasslands are disappearing. Many have been turned into farms. Farm animals harm the grasses by overgrazing. Towns and cities have been built on grasslands too. Climate change also affects grasslands. Some grasslands become deserts as weather patterns become hotter and drier.

In 2019, a wildfire destroyed more than 2.9 million acres (1.2 million ha) of grasslands and forests in South America.

Controlled burns of grasslands can reduce the risk of dangerous wildfires and keep the biomes healthy.

Fire is important to both types of grasslands. Most animals can burrow, fly, or flee from fire. Fire kills the seedlings of most trees and shrubs. It keeps them from taking over the grassland.

The dry grasses aboveground are burned too. But their underground roots are unharmed. The fire burns dead materials on the ground. It releases nutrients from these materials. More sunlight reaches the ground. As a result, grasses regrow easily. Fire helps keep grasslands healthy.

Further Evidence

Visit the website below. Read the text and watch the videos. What new information did you learn about grasslands?

Open Ecosystems

abdocorelibrary.com/grassland-biomes

The bison is the largest land mammal in the United States.

CHAPTER 3

GRASSLAND PLANTS AND ANIMALS

Grasslands are home to many plants and animals. Many hoofed animals depend on grasslands for food and **habitat**. In temperate grasslands, these animals include bison, pronghorn, bighorn sheep, and elk.

Pronghorn herds can grow to include 1,000 individuals.

Gazelles, wildebeests, and zebras are hoofed animals that are found on savannas.

Hoofed animals often live in herds. They are herbivores. This means they eat mainly plants. Their grazing limits the growth of trees and shrubs. This gets rid of competition. Grasses have more sunlight, nutrients, space, and water. This keeps the grasses healthy.

Hoofed animals help grasslands in other ways. Their hooves loosen the soil when they walk. This lets in oxygen and water. It stirs in nutrients. It pushes seeds into the soil. The dung of hoofed animals is good for the soil too.

Surviving Wildfires

Grasslands are full of plant life even belowground. Plant roots run deep underground. This helps them get water during droughts. Deep roots are far away from the hot temperatures of wildfires, helping plants survive. After a fire, new growth sprouts from the roots.

European hares live in grasslands of Europe, Asia, and North America.

Other Grassland Species

Many types of grasses and wildflowers thrive in healthy soil. These plants attract **pollinators**, such as bees and butterflies. Other insects live

Ring-necked pheasants can be found on the Great Plains. Male pheasants, *right*, are more brightly colored than females, *left*.

on the grasslands too. Many types of songbirds are part of grassland biomes. They feed on insects and seeds.

Burrowing owls live underground in burrows made by other grassland animals.

Grasslands also have burrowing animals. Some, such as prairie dogs in North America, dig their own burrows. Many types of insects and reptiles also dig burrows. Burrows allow more air and water into the soil. They provide shelter. Some snakes and owls use empty burrows made by other animals.

Food Web on the Great Plains

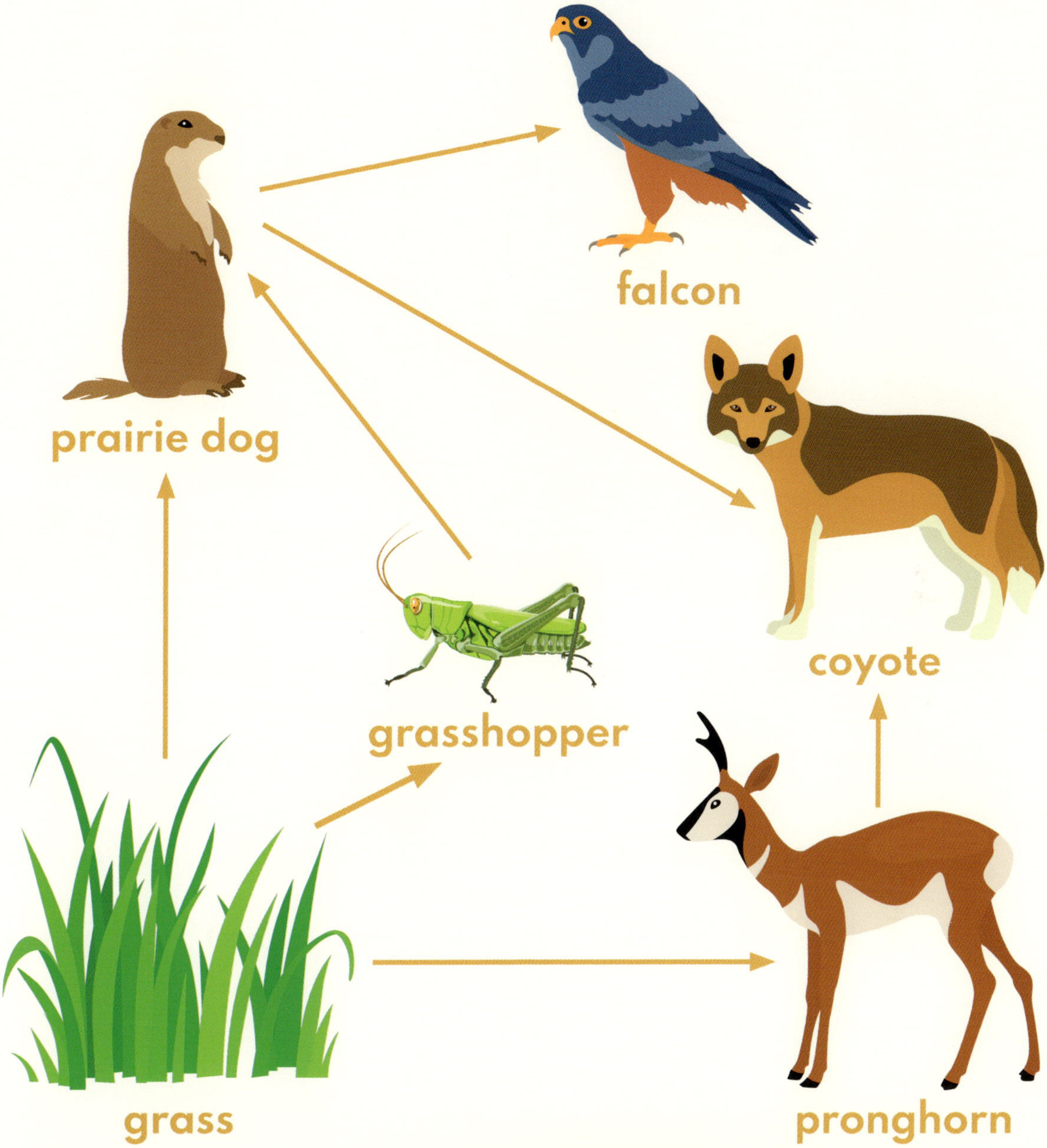

This food web shows the interactions between animals and plants on the Great Plains. The arrows show the flow of nutrients.

Wolves live and hunt together in groups called packs.

Predators hunt many of the hoofed and small animals. Lions and leopards stalk animals on the savanna. Coyotes and wolves hunt on the Great Plains. **Scavengers** such as vultures feast on any remains.

Each plant and animal in the grasslands has a special role. They keep grassland biomes healthy. A healthy grassland supports biodiversity.

PRIMARY SOURCE

Martha Kauffman works for the World Wildlife Fund. She is the managing director of the northern Great Plains program. She explained the importance of grasslands:

> Right here in America is one of the world's most threatened natural systems. The northern Great Plains is as important as the Amazon or Arctic and deserves our attention.

Source: "Northern Great Plains." *World Wildlife Fund*, n.d., worldwildlife.org. Accessed 16 Sept. 2022.

What's the Big Idea?

Read this quote carefully. What is its main idea? Explain how the main idea is supported by details.

EXPLORE THE BIOME

Many plants and animals help make up grassland biomes. Can you identify which parts of this grassland biome are plants? Which are animals? Can you find any nonliving parts of the biome?

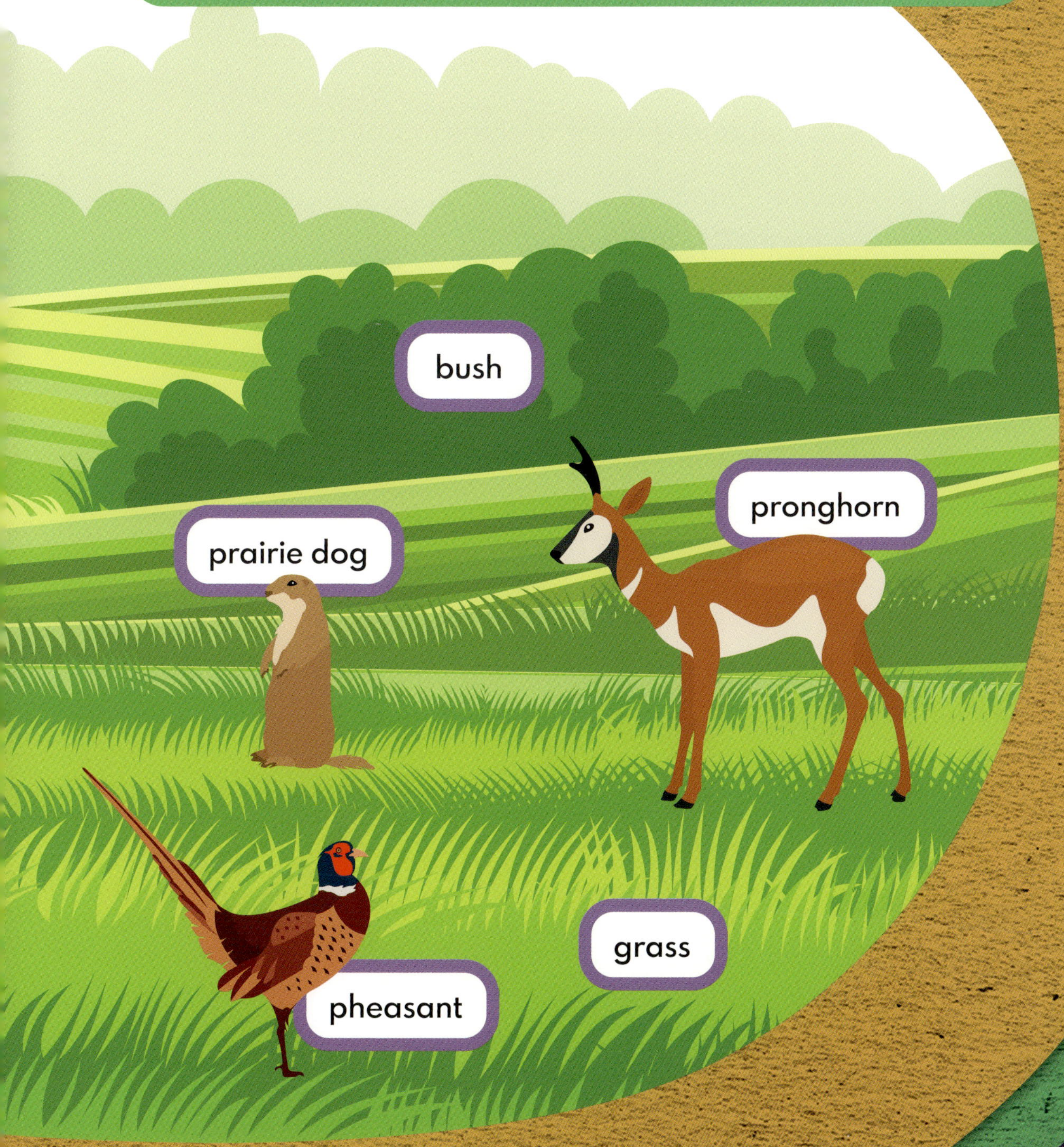

Glossary

adapted
adjusted to survive in a certain biome

biodiversity
the variety of plant and animal species in an area

habitat
a place where animals and plants are naturally found

nutrients
materials that living things need in order to grow and stay alive

pollinators
animals that move pollen from one flower to another

precipitation
liquid or frozen water that falls from the sky, including rain, sleet, and snow

predators
animals that hunt other animals

scavengers
animals that feed on dead animals

Online Resources

To learn more about grassland biomes, visit our free resource websites below.

Core Library CONNECTION
FREE! COMMON CORE MULTIMEDIA RESOURCES

Visit **abdocorelibrary.com** or scan this QR code for free Common Core resources for teachers and students, including vetted activities, multimedia, and booklinks, for deeper subject comprehension.

Booklinks NONFICTION NETWORK
FREE! ONLINE NONFICTION RESOURCES

Visit **abdobooklinks.com** or scan this QR code for free additional online weblinks for further learning. These links are routinely monitored and updated to provide the most current information available.

Learn More

Dickmann, Nancy. *Map and Track Grasslands.* Crabtree, 2019.

Huddleston, Emma. *Food Chains.* Abdo, 2022.

London, Martha. *Ecosystems.* Abdo, 2022.

Index

About the Author

Laura Perdew is a mom, a writing consultant, and an author of more than 50 books for children. She writes both fiction and nonfiction with a focus on nature, the environment, and environmental issues. She lives and plays in Boulder, Colorado.